# Teaching With Favorite
# Dr. Seuss Books

BY JOAN NOVELLI

NEW YORK • TORONTO • LONDON • AUCKLAND • SYDNEY
MEXICO CITY • NEW DELHI • HONG KONG • BUENOS AIRES

SCHOLASTIC
Teaching
Resources

Information for "Meet Dr. Seuss" was excerpted from *The Big Book of Picture-Book Authors and Illustrators* by James Preller. Copyright © 2001 by James Preller.

Interior design by Kathy Massaro
Interior illustrations by Maxie Chambliss, except page 12 by Shelley Dieterichs.

ISBN 0-439-29462-2
Copyright © 2003 by Joan Novelli.
Published by Scholastic Inc.
All rights reserved.
Printed in the U.S.A.

2 3 4 5 6 7 8 9 10    40    09 08 07 06 05 04 03

# Contents

# About This Book

Up, down, dish, fish, yes, mess, tall, all…Dr. Seuss books turn everyday words into magical, memorable adventures. Who can forget the irrepressible Cat in the Hat, who knows how to have "lots of good fun that is funny"? (For starters, this cat can stand on a ball while he holds up a cup and a cake, TWO books, a fish, and various other objects. He can also hop on that ball—and that's not all!) Then there's the compassionate elephant in *Horton Hears a Who!*, whose steadfast belief in the very small citizens of the very tiny town of *Who*-ville saves them from disaster. And, of course, there's the exuberant Mr. Fox (*Fox in Socks*), who plays tricks with bricks, blocks, and clocks to completely confuse Mr. Knox (and many readers). These and other captivating characters bring young readers back again and again, strengthening literacy skills and a love of reading that can last a lifetime.

Wordplay is one of the best ways to encourage literacy skills, making Dr. Seuss books a perfect teaching tool. Whether a Dr. Seuss story is all about silliness, such as *Fox in Socks*, or has a message to share, such as *The Lorax*, the language is unfailingly fun. Children quickly learn to chime in on the rollicking rhymes that take them from beginning to end. This book builds on that wordplay with activities that support the language arts standards for reading, writing, speaking, and listening. For each of the 12 titles featured in this book, a Before You Read activity encourages students to use meaning clues (such as the title and cover) and make predictions about the story. Discussion Starters for each title invite children to respond to questions as they explore characters, setting, and problems; make inferences; and connect the story to their own experiences. Examples of other activities that support the language arts standards include:

◎ What Do You See? (page 12): A fun graphic organizer challenges children to plan the beginning, middle, and end of a story that might top one by Dr. Seuss!

◎ A Dr. Seuss Dictionary (page 15): Children become picture dictionary authors to deepen their understanding of a story.

◎ Oom-pah, Boom-pah (page 20): This word wall reinforces structural analysis (spelling patterns) to build reading and writing skills.

◎ How Exciting Is That! (page 25): This revealing activity explores story structure (sequence of events) and introduces students to a prewriting strategy they can use to make their own writing more powerful.

◎ Counting On Sight Words (page 33): This activity reinforces recognition of sight words.

◎ Mini Beginning-Reader (page 46): Children combine words and pictures to experiment with rhyme in their writing.

◎ Meet These Feet! (page 56): Children discover how adjectives make writing more descriptive with an activity that builds on language patterns in the book.

◎ Stopping the Chopping (page 62): This mapping activity invites children to retell a story in pictures, using sequencing and inferencing skills to capture the important events.

◎ And much more!

Dr. Seuss books are a natural for enhancing other areas of the curriculum, too—especially math. Additional activities in this book support the math standards, building skills with number and operations, shapes and patterns, time and measurement, data analysis, reasoning, and more. For example, *One Fish, Two Fish, Red Fish, Blue Fish* invites skip-counting and multiplying with creatures that have two, four, six, and more feet. (See page 38.)

It's been decades since Dr. Seuss made his debut, and children of all ages continue to be enchanted by his timeless tales. Young children are delighted by the words and pictures, which work together to bring success to early reading experiences. Older readers enjoy revisiting their favorite Seuss stories, and will learn from them in new ways each time. The activities in this book can help bring the spirit of Dr. Seuss into the classroom and inspire lasting literature-based learning that is full of fun.

# Connections to the Language Arts Standards

The activities in this book are designed to support you in meeting the following standards outlined by the Mid-continent Research for Education and Learning (McREL), an organization that collects and synthesizes national and state K–12 curriculum standards.

## Language Arts

**Uses the general skills and strategies of the reading process and reading skills and strategies to understand and interpret a variety of literary texts:**

◆ Uses basic elements of phonetic analysis (for example, common letter-sound relationships and vowel sounds) to decode unknown words

◆ Uses basic elements of structural analysis (for example, compound words and spelling patterns) to decode unknown words

◆ Understands level-appropriate sight words and vocabulary (for example, high-frequency words such as *said*, *was*, and *where*)

◆ Reads aloud familiar stories, poems, and passages with fluency and expression (for example, rhythm, tone, intonation)

◆ Uses meaning clues (for example, title and cover) to aid comprehension and make predictions about content

◆ Knows main ideas or theme, setting, main characters, main events, sequence, and problems in stories

◆ Makes simple inferences regarding the order of events and possible outcomes

◆ Relates stories to personal experience

**Uses the general skills and strategies of the writing process and uses grammatical and mechanical conventions in written compositions:**

◆ Uses prewriting strategies to plan written work (for example, discusses ideas with peers)

◆ Uses strategies to organize written work (for example, includes a beginning, middle, and ending; uses sequence of events)

◆ Uses writing and other methods (for example, drawing pictures, telling, and making lists) to describe familiar persons, places, objects, or experiences

◆ Writes in a variety of forms or genres (for example, picture books, stories, and responses to literature)

◆ Uses declarative and interrogative sentences in written compositions

◆ Uses nouns and adjectives in written compositions

◆ Uses conventions of spelling in written compositions (for example, letter-sound relationships)

◆ Uses conventions of punctuation

**Uses listening and speaking strategies for different purposes:**

◆ Makes contributions in class and group discussions

◆ Asks and responds to questions

◆ Recites and responds to familiar stories, poems, and rhymes with patterns (for example, retells in sequence; relates information to own life; describes characters, setting, plot)

Source: *Content Knowledge: A Compendium of Standards and Benchmarks for K–12 Education* (3rd ed.). Mid-continent Research for Education and Learning, 2000.

# Meet Dr. Seuss

## Born: March 2, 1904, in Springfield, Massachusetts

Where did Dr. Seuss get the idea for an elephant hatching an egg in a tree? How did he come up with all those inventive names for the imaginative characters in his stories? Find the answers to these and other intriguing questions in the following information.

### Is Dr. Seuss his real name?

Dr. Seuss wasn't the author's birth name; it's a pseudonym invented by the writer. His real name was Theodor Seuss Geisel (GUY-zel).

### Where did Dr. Seuss get all of his wonderfully wacky ideas?

"Anything can spark an idea," Seuss said. And believe it or not, once an idea blew in through an open window. Seuss was at his drawing table, aimlessly doodling. Suddenly, a gentle breeze blew a drawing he had made of an elephant on top of another drawing he had made of a tree. Seuss remembered, "I said to myself, an elephant in a tree! What's he doing there? Finally I said to myself, Of course! He's hatching an egg!" Seuss had discovered the idea for his next book, *Horton Hatches an Egg*.

### Did the art or story come first for Dr. Seuss?

For Seuss, doodling was a favorite technique used to conjure up ideas. For example, he once drew a picture of a turtle sitting on top of another turtle. Seuss kept drawing until there was a huge pile of turtles stacked one on top of the other. He looked at the preposterous pile of turtles and asked himself, "Why? What does this mean?" (To discover how Seuss answered this question, you'll have to read *Yertle the Turtle and Other Stories*!)

### How did Dr. Seuss come up with all those weird names, like Bartholomew Cubbins, the Zooks and the Sneetches, the Grinch, the Tufted Gustard, and the Lorax?

"That's the easy part," Seuss claimed. "I can look at an animal and know what it is."

### When did Dr. Seuss first become interested in animals?

Seuss's interest in animals blossomed when he was just a little boy and his father ran a zoo in Massachusetts. Seuss would visit with a sketchpad, stand outside the cages, and draw all the animals. Of course, he drew them his own way!

Dr. Seuss passed away September 24, 1991, at the age of 87. During his life, Dr. Seuss wrote and illustrated more than 44 books! How many of these can your students name? How many can they read?

The information in this profile was excerpted from *The Big Book of Picture-Book Authors and Illustrators* by James Preller (Scholastic, 2001).

# A Seuss Celebration

The year 2004 marks the 100th birthday of Dr. Seuss! Whether you're teaching with Dr. Seuss stories in honor of this special occasion, or enjoying them with students just because they're always a favorite and full of teaching opportunities, children will enjoy a festive celebration that is as colorful and creative as these best-loved books. Following are a few ideas to enliven your classroom celebration of Dr. Seuss.

## Party Hats

Dr. Seuss stories have some hats that are as unique as the characters wearing them. For starters, there's the tall red-and-white striped hat worn by the Cat in the Hat, and the hat with a hook and a book about how to cook worn by the Nook (in *One Fish, Two Fish, Red Fish, Blue Fish*). Revisit Dr. Seuss stories to notice other hats. Then let children design and make their own. A brown paper grocery bag with the top rolled down a few times makes a good hat. (Pinch and tape sides for a snug fit.) Paint and decorate with curly ribbon, sequins, and other craft materials for a special look. For another fun hat, staple a wide strip of tagboard to make a headband. Attach pipe cleaners around the edges. Add curly ribbon, colorful pompoms, tissue paper flowers, and other decorations.

## Seuss Snacks

Let children revisit Dr. Seuss books to plan a snack menu for a celebration. How about "Beezle-Nut" juice (from *Horton Hears a Who!*), frankfurter roasts and marshmallow toasts (from *The Sneetches*), noodles (from *Fox in Socks*), Truffula Fruits (from *The Lorax*), and, of course, green eggs and ham (from *Green Eggs and Ham*).

## Dr. Seuss Read-a-Thon

Host a schoolwide Dr. Seuss Read-a-Thon. How many stories written and illustrated by Dr. Seuss can the students in your school read? Write each title on a large sheet of paper. Display it in the school library, cafeteria, or lobby. Have classes check off books as they read them. Can your school get at least one check next to each title? Take a schoolwide vote: Which book is the all-time favorite?

## And the Award Goes to...

Invite children to create awards for favorite Dr. Seuss books. They might make certificates, posters, or models in honor of their award winners, and they can announce them to the class and share a short speech. Provide a microphone (real or pretend) to set the tone for this important occasion.

# Literacy Activities for Any Time

## Tip
▲▲▲▲▲

Encourage a playful approach to language by exploring rhyming dictionaries and online rhyming resources with students.

● *Scholastic Rhyming Dictionary,* by Sue Young (Scholastic, 1997). This child-friendly reference book is organized by vowel sounds and final syllables and features more than 15,000 words.

● *RhymeZone* (www.rhymezone.com). This site makes it easy to rhyme with even the toughest of words. Find fun rhymes for easy words, too—for example, type in *cat,* and choose from more than 200 rhyming words, including *hat, gnat, rat-a-tat,* and *little brown bat!*

Dr. Seuss stories are full of invitations to build literacy skills. Rhyming words teach vowel sounds, reinforce spelling patterns, build sight vocabulary, and more. Lively language enriches learning about word choice, syntax, and conventions of language. Colorful characters keep the stories going and offer opportunities to explore dialogue, onomatopoeia, alliteration, story structure, and more.

## Mystery Words

The rhyming words in Dr. Seuss stories make them perfect for activities that build sight vocabulary. Try this mystery word activity to help children make connections between the language they hear and the words they see.

◎ After sharing a Dr. Seuss story, write pairs of sentences on sentence strips. Use a large sticky note to cover one of the rhyming words at the end of a line.

◎ Together, read the lines aloud, pointing to each word as you say it.

◎ When you get to the covered word, ask children to predict what the word is. Lift the sticky note to let them check their guesses.

## Skill-Building Displays

Use Dr. Seuss stories as inspiration for playful displays that build vocabulary and enhance writing skills. Following are several ideas:

◎ Ask children to be on the lookout for words that sound like their meaning. Some examples are *oom-pahs, toots,* and *chirp* (from *Horton Hears a Who!*) and *plop, bump,* and *thump* (from *The Cat in the Hat*). Build a word wall with such words and introduce the term *onomatopoeia.* Children can illustrate the word wall to add visual clues.

◎ Invite children to listen for alliterative language in the story. After reading, revisit some of the alliteration in the story. Let children have fun saying the words with emphasis on the repeating sounds—such as "Ben bends Bin's broom," from *Fox in Socks.* Create a display for children to post favorite alliterative lines. Encourage them to use the display as a writing resource.

◎ Let students practice the conventions of dialogue in their writing by playing with some of the dialogue from Dr. Seuss stories. Copy dialogue on sentence strips. Cut apart the quotation marks, punctuation, and dialogue tags. Use Velcro to attach the pieces to tagboard. Place the materials at a center, and let children put sentences together to show who says what.

## Guess Who!

Dr. Seuss stories feature some of the most memorable characters in children's literature. There's Horton, who lives in the Jungle of Nool, the Cat in the Hat and his trademark tricks, Sam and his green eggs and ham, the Sneetches—both the Star-Belly and Plain-Belly sort—Yertle the Turtle whose kingly ambitions go a little too far, and more. Explore the characters in various Dr. Seuss stories with this guessing game:

◎ Invite children to choose a favorite character. Ask children to pretend to be that character and write a set of clues that describes who they are. Have them start with general clues and get progressively more specific—for example, *I live in a jungle. I like to swim. I have a trunk. I have big ears. I am determined. I searched a big field of clovers for my small friends. I found them on the last clover and kept them safe.*

◎ Let children take turns reading aloud their clues one at a time, giving classmates a chance to guess their identity after each clue.

## Story Maps

Creating a map of a story challenges children to make connections between characters, setting, and events.

◎ Have children brainstorm characters and places in a story. List these on the chalkboard or chart paper.

◎ Model the activity by making a map that incorporates children's suggestions. Then let children make their own map, generating a list of characters and places for a Dr. Seuss story and incorporating them in a map.

◎ Have children use what they know about the setting to make inferences and fill in the details of a map. For example, in *And to Think That I Saw It on Mulberry Street*, the boy describes what he sees on his way to and from school. The school is never pictured, but children can infer that he arrives and include the school on their map.

## The Dr. Seuss Picture Dictionary

Learn about all sorts of words—even the made-up kind—with this activity.

◎ As you share Dr. Seuss stories, have children look for words the author makes up—for example, *moof, miff-muffered, gruvvulous, rippulous, snergelly,* and *snarggled* (all from *The Lorax*). Write the words on chart paper.

◎ Invite children to choose a word from the list to add to a picture dictionary. Have them write the word on paper, illustrate it, and then write a definition. Then have children help arrange the pages in alphabetical order. Bind with O-rings or paper fasteners so it's easy to add new pages.

# And to Think That I Saw It on Mulberry Street

(RANDOM HOUSE, 1937;
RENEWED 1964)

Imagination runs wild in this book about a boy on his way to school and back home again. What did he see? A horse and wagon is just the beginning!

## Before You Read

What kind of a street is Mulberry Street? Share the cover with children and ask them to describe it. They'll notice that there's not a lot of detail. They won't see trees, shops, houses, cars, or other things they might expect to see on a street. Use this observation to discuss why this is a good picture for the cover. (Readers can use their imagination, just like the boy in the story, to bring this street to life.)

## After You Read

Discussion Starters

What a story the boy has to tell about Mulberry Street! It becomes more and more inventive as the story goes on. Use these questions to guide a discussion that invites students to explore character, setting, and story structure.

◎ What are some words that describe the boy in the story?

◎ The boy travels a "long way" to and from school. How far do you think that is?

◎ What pattern do you notice in the boy's story? (*Each time the boy adds something to the story, he discovers there's a need for something else. For example, he adds the band, and then a trailer to sit in, and then a couple more animals to help pull the heavier load. One thing leads to another.*)

◎ What do you think the father might have said to the boy at the end (when the father asks what the boy saw and the boy says "Nothing")?

◎ Did the ending surprise you? Why?

## What's That Word? (Language Arts)

The boy's descriptions of what he sees offer lots of opportunities to build vocabulary and use of context clues.

◉ Reread the story, asking children to listen for words that are new to them.

◉ Write new vocabulary on chart paper—for example, *sternly, keen, outlandish, chariot, marvelous, rumbling, fleet, Rajah, hitched,* and *Aldermen.*

◉ Reread the sentences that include these words. Ask children what they think each word means. Encourage them to share the clues they used to guess the meaning.

◉ Play a game with the words to reinforce meaning. Write a sentence that uses one of the new words on the chalkboard. Leave a blank in place of the word. Can students guess which word belongs?

◉ Let children take turns coming up with sentences to challenge their classmates. Have them write the sentences on paper, leaving blanks for the new words. Collect the papers. Read the sentences aloud, letting children chime in on the missing words.

## Simile Mixup (Language Arts and Movement)

Ask children to recall what the chariot rumbles like down Mulberry Street (thunder). Use this simile to teach a mini-lesson on descriptive language. Follow up with a game that lets children put mixed-up similes back together.

◉ Reread the description of the chariot "rumbling like thunder." Invite students to tell what thunder sounds like. Is *rumble* a good word to describe thunder? What would a chariot rumbling sound like? Invite students to imitate the sound it might make.

◉ Explain that comparisons that use *like* or *as* are called similes. Share other examples of similes, and let students make up some of their own—for example, "A night without homework is like summer vacation."

◉ Play a game of mixed-up similes to strengthen students' understanding. Write similes on sentence strips. Cut them apart between the beginning ("A night without homework is like…") and ending ("…summer vacation.") Mix up the beginnings and endings and give one to each child. Have children find a partner to make a complete simile with. Let children share their similes with the class. Don't be surprised if the similes are set up a little differently once students put them back together, but that will add to the fun.

Book Link

For another story about an imaginative journey to school, share **The Secret Shortcut**, by Mark Teague (Scholastic, 1996). Wendell and Floyd just can't get themselves to school on time and the stories they tell get bigger and bigger. When their frustrated teacher finally tells them "Be here on time tomorrow—or else! And no more crazy excuses!" they come up with a foolproof shortcut, one that takes them on their wildest adventure of all!

Tip

▲▲▲▲▲

For more practice with similes, include the beginning of one in a morning message—for example, "Having double recess is like _____ ." At morning meeting, let students take turns completing the simile.

## What Do You See? (Language Arts)

The boy has a story "that NO ONE could beat!" But students will have fun trying!

◎ Revisit the end of the story. If he wasn't quite home, what else might the boy see on Mulberry Street?

◎ Invite children to rewrite the ending, taking turns adding to what the boy saw to make it a story that really can't be beat.

◎ Go further by letting children make up outlandish tales about what they see on their way to school. Give each child a copy of page 13. Ask children to cut out the street, street sign, and story boxes. Have them arrange and glue the pieces on a sheet of drawing paper, placing the story boxes (beginning, middle, ending) in order from left to right. Students are now ready to write and illustrate their stories!

## Street Safety (Health & Safety, Art, and Movement)

With everything from a zebra and reindeer to an elephant and airplane, Mulberry Street is a busy place! Use this lively story as a springboard for a safety lesson.

◎ Invite students to describe Mulberry Street: What did the boy see?

◎ Display a large sheet of mural paper. Make a Mulberry Street sign for the mural. Then let students use their imagination to show what they see on Mulberry Street.

◎ Ask students to tell what safety rules they think the boy followed on Mulberry Street. For example, did he stay on the sidewalk? If he had to cross the street, did he wait for the crossing sign and look both ways?

◎ Use colorful electrical tape to mark off a street next to the mural. Then let students practice crossing Mulberry Street! Sing a piggyback song (left) to help children remember to look both ways.

## Tip

▲▲▲▲▲

For dozens of health and safety lessons, see *Fresh & Fun: Health and Safety,* by Deborah Rovin-Murphy and Frank Murphy (Scholastic, 2001).

### Stop, Look, and Listen

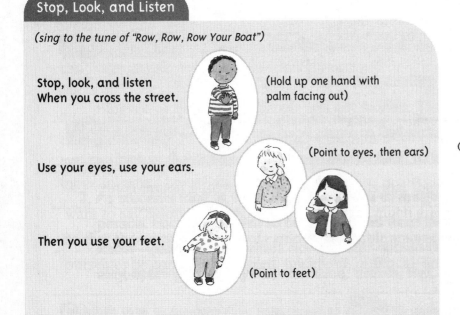

*(sing to the tune of "Row, Row, Row Your Boat")*

Stop, look, and listen
When you cross the street.

(Hold up one hand with palm facing out)

(Point to eyes, then ears)

Use your eyes, use your ears.

Then you use your feet.

(Point to feet)

# What Do You See?

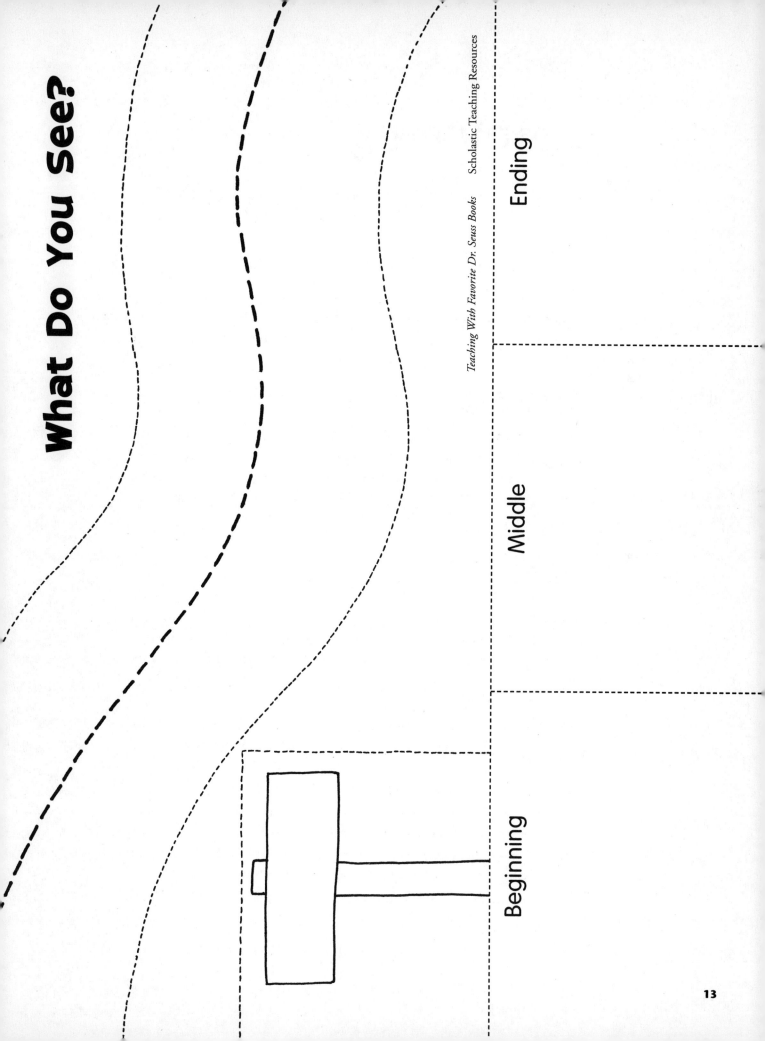

Beginning

Middle

Ending

# Bartholomew and the Oobleck

(RANDOM HOUSE, 1949;
RENEWED 1976)

A page boy named Bartholomew proves himself wiser than a mighty ruler, and saves the kingdom from being swallowed up by buckets of gooey, green goop.

## Before You Read

*Oobleck* may be a familiar word to children, many of whom may have plunged their hands into a water table filled with the irresistibly sticky stuff. Let children share their experiences with the substance. Set the stage for this fanciful story by giving each child a handful of oobleck. (For a recipe, see page 15.) Let children squish and squeeze as you read.

## After You Read

In addition to being a wonderful springboard to a discussion about the seasons, this story contains gentle lessons about restraint, responsibility, and remorse. Explore these ideas while learning more about the story's characters with the following questions.

◎ Why wasn't the king satisfied with the spring rains, summer sunshine, autumn fog, and winter snow that came down from the sky every year?

◎ What do you think Bartholomew meant when he said "even kings can't rule the *sky*." Why do you think the king didn't listen?

◎ What words do you think best describe the king? What words do you think best describe Bartholomew? (Have children explain their choices.)

◎ Can you think of another way the king could have solved the problem of being tired of the same four things coming down from the sky?

◎ Why were the four things that came down from the sky (rain, sun, fog, snow) "perfect" in the end?

## A Dr. Seuss Dictionary (Language Arts)

Dr. Seuss stories are full of plenty of new vocabulary—including many words children won't find in a dictionary. They can guess what some words, such as *glugg* and *gloing*, mean—they sound like their meaning. They can guess what other words, such as *oobleck*, mean from story descriptions. Use this activity to have fun with these words and practice dictionary skills.

◉ On chart paper, write words from the story that children won't find in a dictionary (such as *glugg, gloing,* and *oobleck*).

◉ Model dictionary skills as you look up each word. Guide children to notice the words at the top of each dictionary page (and the purpose they serve). Review alphabetical order (and how this makes it easier to locate words), and how pictures help show what some words mean.

◉ Give each child a copy of page 17. Invite children to become dictionary authors by completing the entries for each word. Have them work in pairs to find the page in the dictionary where each word would be located and record the guide words at the top. Have them continue by writing a definition for each word and drawing a picture that shows the meaning. Children can complete page four with a word of their choice from the story, and then cut out the pages and put them together to make a mini-book.

## I'm an Oobleck Scientist! (Math, Science, and Language Arts)

Use children's enthusiasm for oobleck to practice writing and following directions.

◉ Ask children how they could make oobleck. Let them quietly think about the question and then write directions for making it.

◉ Read aloud children's directions. What do the directions have in common? How are they different?

◉ Share a recipe for oobleck with students. (See right.) How is it like their recipes? How is it different?

◉ Follow the directions with students to mix up a batch of oobleck. Scoop some into a resealable sandwich bag for each child. Explore the properties of this gooey, sticky, stretchy stuff. For example, challenge children to break off grape seed–size blobs. Does the oobleck hold its shape? Can students stretch it? Snap it like a rubber band?

◉ Invite students to use their senses to learn more. Give each child a copy of page 18. Have students use their sense of sight, touch, smell, and hearing to investigate this irresistible substance. Discuss students' observations. Ask: "Based on your observations, do you think oobleck is a solid or liquid?" (*Oobleck has properties of both.*)

# Oobleck
▲▲▲▲▲

Pour 3 cups room-temperature water into a large bowl. Add 5–6 drops green food coloring. Stir in 5 cups cornstarch (one cup at a time) and mix well. Adjust the mixture as needed by adding more water or cornstarch.

## Acting Out With Oobleck (Language Arts and Math)

Oobleck came down from the sky in blobs that ranged from grape seed– to football-size. What would that look like? Find out!

◉ Ask students to recall what the blobs of oobleck were compared to—from smallest to biggest (grape seeds, cupcakes, baseballs, footballs). Record the comparison words on chart paper.

◉ Bring in the objects. Let students display them in size order. Brainstorm other things that are about the same size. For example, mini-chocolate chips might be about the same size as grape seeds. A loaf of bread might be about as big as a football.

◉ Give each child some oobleck. (See recipe, page 15.) Have children shape the oobleck to make different-sized blobs. (They won't be the same sizes as the blobs in the story, but students can represent them with smaller blobs of increasing sizes.) Reread the story as children make the oobleck fall down from the sky at the appropriate times. (For easy cleanup, cover desks or floor space with newspaper.)

## Where *Is* That Kingdom? (Science and Geography)

Judging from the rain, sun, fog, and snow that come down from the sky every year, could the Kingdom of Didd be nearby? Explore the relationship between geography and weather with this activity.

◉ Chart seasonal weather conditions for your region. Compare these with the weather the king observes. How are they alike? How are they different?

◉ Ask students to decide, based on their comparisons, if the Kingdom of Didd could be located near them. Encourage them to explain their reasoning.

◉ If students decide the Kingdom of Didd could not be nearby, have them use weather maps and reports to determine possible locations. If it is nearby, what other places share similar seasonal weather conditions and would be a possible location for the kingdom?

Tip

▲▲▲▲▲

To follow the weather near and far, go to **www.accuweather.com**.

glugg: _____

_____

_____

gloing: _____

_____

_____

oobleck: _____

_____

_____

_____: _____

_____

_____

Name _____  Date _____

# ⭐ I'm an Oobleck Scientist! ⭐

Scientists use their senses to learn about the world around them. Use your sense of sight, touch, hearing, and smell to learn about oobleck!

Look at the oobleck. Record three things about the way oobleck looks.

_____

_____

_____

Touch the oobleck. Record three things about the way oobleck feels.

_____

_____

_____

Smell the oobleck. Record three things about the way oobleck smells.

_____

_____

_____

Stretch the oobleck. Drop it on the table. Pull off bits of oobleck. Record three things about what you hear. (You can make up words for the sounds you hear!)

_____

_____

_____

**Be a Super Scientist!**

**Is oobleck a solid, like an apple or a book, or is it a liquid, like milk or water?**

I think that oobleck is a _____ because

_____.

Teaching With Favorite Dr. Seuss Books · Scholastic Teaching Resources

# Horton Hears a Who!

(RANDOM HOUSE, 1954, RENEWED 1982)

**H**orton the elephant hears a small noise, and discovers the town of *Who*-ville atop a speck of dust. Horton sets out to protect the creatures of this tiny town, and he doesn't let anything get in the way of his convictions.

## Before You Read

The word *who* is usually used as an interrogative pronoun to ask a question—for example, "*Who* is Horton?" But in this story, *who* is a noun, and Horton hears one! Just what does a Who sound like? Let children take turns sharing their ideas before reading the story.

## After You Read

This fast-paced story has all the elements of a great adventure. Explore the story structure of an adventure, and build comprehension skills with the questions that follow:

◎ What happens at the beginning that makes you want to keep reading?

◎ Who is the hero in this story? What are some qualities that make this character a hero?

◎ Where does Horton live? What kinds of things might you find there? Who are Horton's neighbors?

◎ What is the big problem in this story?

◎ What are some ways Horton tries to solve the problem? What happens each time?

◎ When Horton says "A person's a person, no matter how small," what do you think he means?

Add to the wall as children discover new double -*o* words in their reading or writing.

## Oom-pah, Boom-pah

(Language Arts)

*Nool, cool, pool...* there are three double -*o* words on the very first page! On other pages, children can find *oom-pahs, boom-pahs, hallabaloo,* and more! Focus on this spelling pattern with an illustrated double -*o* word wall.

◉ List double -*o* words from the book on the chalkboard or chart paper. Brainstorm other double -*o* words, such as *school, tool, spool, boom, zoom, broom, moon, soon, noon, goose, loose, moose, boot, toot, scoot, ooze,* and *snooze.* Have children group the words by vowel sound.

◉ Give each child a sheet of drawing paper. Have children choose a double -*o* word to write on the paper. Let children have fun turning the double -*o* letters into eyes, apples, faces, or any other suitable art.

◉ Group and display the words by vowel sounds. Take a break every now and then for some "double -*o*" spelling practice. Have children close their eyes or turn their heads away from the wall. Give them words from the wall to practice spelling together. Let them chant each letter, and call out a big "double -*o*!" at the right time.

### *Who? Where? Won't!* (Language Arts)

Provide practice with computer skills by having students type their sentences and choose the italic font style for the designated words.

Horton is a *very* expressive elephant. Revisit some of the words in the book to see just *how* expressive, and explore how using italics helps authors to communicate effectively and for different purposes.

◉ Revisit the story, having students take turns finding and pointing out words in italics. Read aloud one of the sentences with an italicized word. Use plenty of expression to convey the meaning of the italicized word. Reread the sentence with no change of expression for the italicized word. Ask children which way has more meaning.

◉ Ask children to listen for italicized words as you reread the story. Discuss the different ways using italics can help communicate meaning—for example, to express surprise, urgency, insistence, seriousness, and excitement.

◉ Invite children to write their own sentences that use italics for at least one word. Encourage them to look to everyday conversations for ideas—for example, "It's *freezing*!" "I'm *so* excited tomorrow's my birthday!" and "Only *three* more days until vacation."

## Who Is Horton? (Language Arts)

Horton might be an elephant, but he is full of admirable qualities. Explore character development by taking a closer look at this unlikely hero—on the outside and on the inside.

◉ After sharing the story, ask children to think about how they would describe Horton. While they're thinking, set up two sets of stations to record ideas. For the first set of stations, display two sheets of chart paper. Label one "Horton on the Outside." Label the other "Horton on the Inside." Repeat this for the second set of stations. Stock each station with elephant patterns (page 23), markers, and tape.

◉ Divide the class into four groups. Assign each group to a station. On your signal, ask children in each group to brainstorm descriptions that would fit on their chart paper. Have them record their ideas on the elephants and tape them to the chart paper. When you say "Stop," have children move to the next station and repeat the procedure.

◉ Once each group has visited both an "Outside" and "Inside" station, bring the class together and combine the descriptions for each category. Let students share reasons for describing Horton as they did. For example, if a student recorded the word *fair* to describe Horton on the inside, a reason might be that Horton repeats his desire (several times) to protect the creatures, however small they might be. Discuss how what a character says can reveal something about what's on the inside.

◉ Wrap up the activity by letting children share what they know about other characters on the outside and inside. Discuss why it's important for authors to think about both when they write stories.

## Tip
▲▲▲▲▲

Two sets of stations will allow children to record ideas more efficiently. For a small group, one set of stations might be enough.

## Book Link

Learn more about Horton's kind and caring disposition with *Horton Hatches the Egg*, by Dr. Seuss (Random House, 1940). Follow up by writing a class story about Horton. What problem will students have this good-natured elephant solve?

## What's Your Number? Match-Up (Math)

*Horton Hears a Who!* begins on the fifteenth of May. Use this as a springboard to explore different ways of representing numbers.

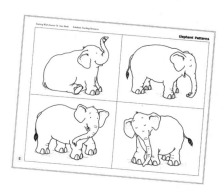

◎ Write the first sentence of the story on the chalkboard. Ask children to identify which words tell when the story begins.

◎ Underline the words *fifteenth of May*. Ask: "If the story began two days earlier, what word would take the place of *fifteenth*?" (*thirteenth*) Write this word on the chalkboard. Let children suggest another way to write the same number.

◎ Repeat the process for other days—for example, ten days earlier, five days later, two weeks later. Write the new numbers on the chalkboard.

◎ Invite children to tell what all of these words show. (*order or position, such as* first, second, *and* third)

◎ Play What's Your Number? to provide practice matching ordinal numbers with numerals. Photocopy the elephant shapes on page 23 (one elephant per child). Write ordinal numbers on half the elephants and the matching numerals on the other half. Mix them up and give one to each child. Have children move around the room, looking for the elephant that makes a match. Once all children have found their matches, let them take turns retelling the beginning of the story, substituting their ordinal number for the word *fifteenth*.

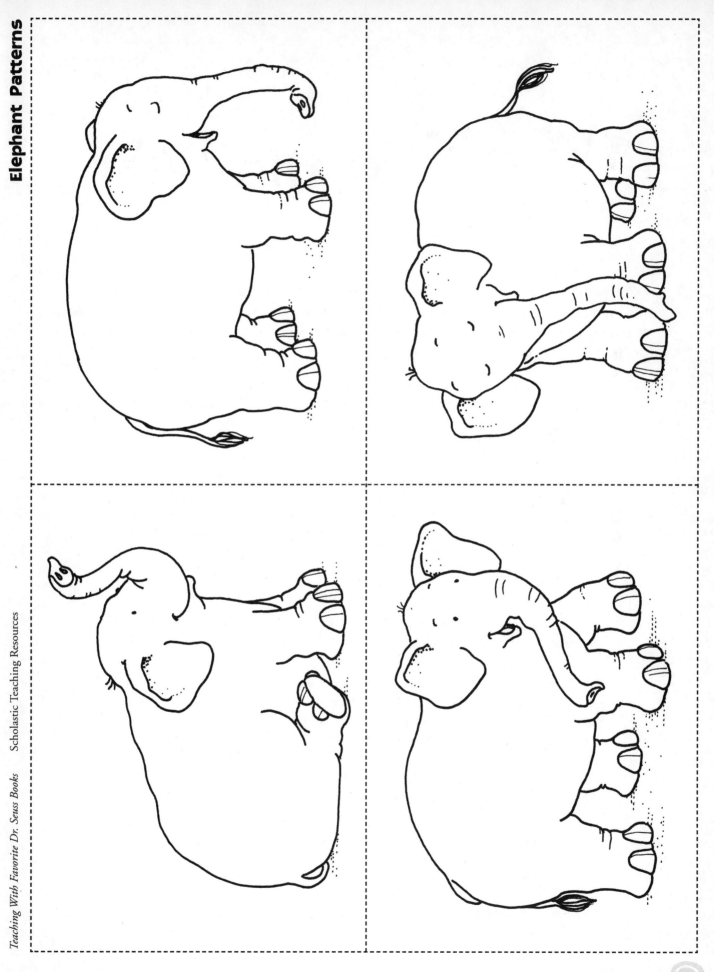

# The Cat in the Hat

(RANDOM HOUSE, 1957; RENEWED 1985)

Two children stare cheerlessly out a window. But not for long! They are soon out of their seats and off on a lively adventure with the Cat in the Hat, who promises all kinds of fun. Of course, the Cat in the Hat's kind of fun comes with a mess that becomes so out of control it will take a really big trick to clean it all up.

## Before You Read

Hold up the cover illustration of *The Cat in the Hat*. To get children in a rhyming (and silly) frame of mind, ask, "What if the cat were a different animal? How about a mouse?" Let children complete the title "The Mouse in the _____" with an article of clothing (such as a *blouse*) to parallel the rhyme in *The Cat in the Hat*. Try the same thing with other animals, such as a goat and bee.

## After You Read

The Cat in the Hat knows some "good games" and "new tricks." Use these questions with children to have more fun with those games and tricks and to explore the colorful characters in this lively story.

◎ What is something that the cat's games and tricks have in common?

◎ What do the cat's expressions tell us about him?

◎ Which game do you think the cat likes best? Why?

◎ Which game do you think Mother would have liked least? Why?

◎ If you could add on to the story, what would you have the children tell their mother?

◎ How do you think parents would feel about the cat visiting while they were away?

## ! ! ! (Language Arts)

This book is full of expression, with exclamation points on almost every page! To help children get a feel for how this punctuation mark can lend expression to a story, try this:

◎ Assign each child an exclamatory sentence in the story. Write each child's line on a sentence strip.

◎ Give children time to practice their lines, with as much expression as the exclamation point indicates.

◎ Gather children in a circle to reread the story. Have children sit in order of their lines, with the child whose line is first sitting to your left.

◎ When you get to the first child's line, signal this child to read the line aloud. Continue, signaling each child in turn to read the lines as they come up in the story.

◎ To extend the activity, let children pair up to write an exclamatory sentence about the story. Have them share the sentences with the class, using their voices to communicate the intended emotion or surprise.

## How Exciting Is That! (Language Arts)

The Cat in the Hat's tricks make for one exciting event after another. Explore story structure by looking at the way all that excitement (and the sequence of events) helps shape the story. Children can use what they learn about plot patterns to effectively organize events in stories they write.

◎ Reread the story, stopping to list each main event.

◎ Revisit each event on the list, asking students to give it an excitement rating from 0 to 5 (with 5 being most exciting).

◎ Plot the ratings in order on a line graph. What pattern do students see? Reinforce the idea of plot patterns by repeating the activity with other stories, including children's own, if they wish to share. Discuss how children can use this idea to make their stories stronger.

### Tip

Make an interactive display that lets children explore the conventions of punctuation. Write sentences from the story on sentence strips, without punctuation. Write corresponding punctuation marks (periods, question marks, exclamation points) on sentence strips and trim to size. Place Velcro at the end of each sentence where punctuation belongs. Place Velcro on the back of each punctuation mark. Let children decide which punctuation works best with each sentence and stick it in place.

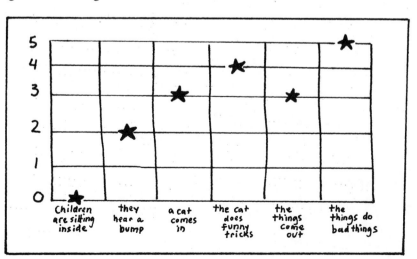

25

Book
Link

Meet up with the Cat in the
Hat again in **The Cat in the
Hat Comes Back**, by Dr.
Seuss (Random House,
1958). This time the cat with
the tricks distracts Sally
and her brother from their
job of shoveling snow.
Sally is wise to this cat's
tricks now, but things can't
help but get a little out of
hand anyway, which gives
the Cat in the Hat a chance
to try out VOOM.

## Dress the Cat (Math and Art)

The Cat in the Hat wears a trademark hat
and tie combination: a red-and-white striped
hat and a red bow tie. Now, what if the Cat
in the Hat got tired of the same old thing
and wanted to try something new?
Experiment with new hats and ties for the
Cat in the Hat, to explore the connection
between combinations and multiplication.

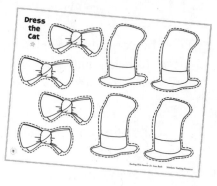

◎ Give each child a copy of the hat and tie patterns on page 27. Have
children color and cut out the hats and ties, making each a different
color and/or pattern. Ask children to color and cut out a cat that could
wear these hats and ties.

◎ Have children dress the cat to find out how many different
combinations of hats and ties they can create.

◎ Once children have had a chance to come up with some ideas about the
number of different combinations, let them share their ideas. Then
guide them to discover that if they multiply the number of hats by the
number of bow ties, they will find out how many combinations are
possible—for example:

- ◆ 1 hat and 1 tie = 1 combination
- ◆ 1 hat and 2 ties = 2 combinations
- ◆ 1 hat and 3 ties = 3 combinations
- ◆ 1 hat and 4 ties = 4 combinations
- ◆ 2 hats and 1 tie = 2 combinations
- ◆ 2 hats and 2 ties = 4 combinations
- ◆ 2 hats and 3 ties = 6 combinations

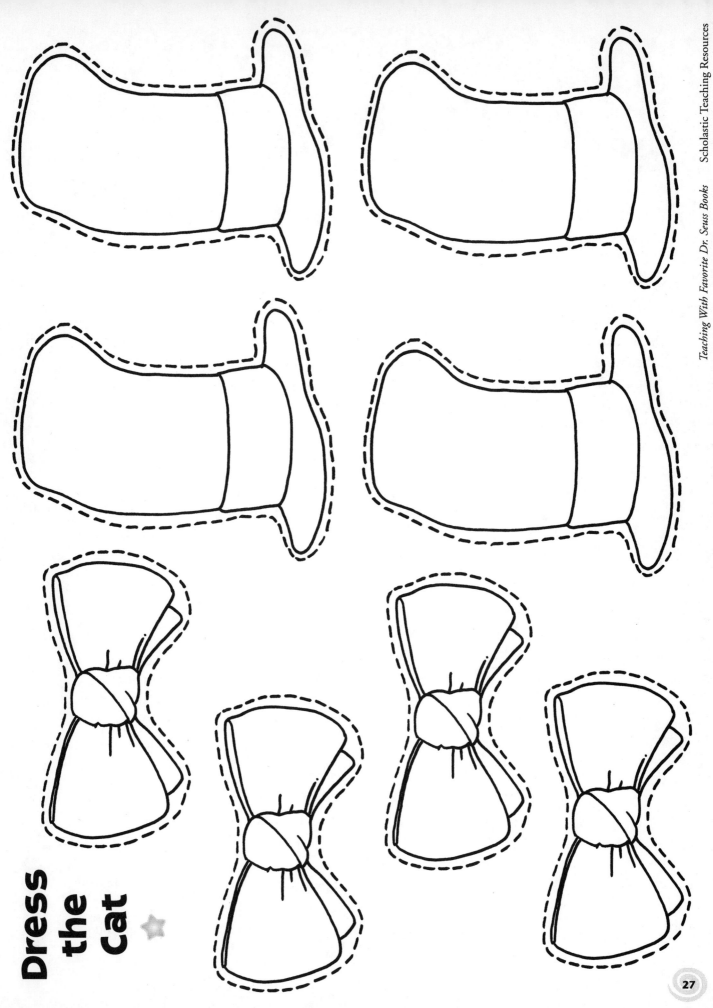

**Dress the Cat** ⭐

Teaching With Favorite Dr. Seuss Books    Scholastic Teaching Resources

# Yertle the Turtle and Other Stories

(RANDOM HOUSE, 1958;
RENEWED 1986)

Yertle the Turtle is king of the pond, but that's not enough. Gertrude McFuzz has a lovely tail, but Lolla-Lee-Lou has two! And Mr. Rabbit and Mr. Bear are both silly enough to believe each other's tall tales about what they can hear and see (until a worm shows them up). Three lively stories teach three lasting lessons that apply as easily to people as they do to the characters in the book.

## Before You Read

Explore rhyme by inviting students to think of other names Dr. Seuss could have chosen for the turtle. How about Mertle the Turtle or Zertle the Turtle? Share the book cover, and ask children to make some predictions: Why is the turtle at the top smiling? Why are the turtles underneath not smiling? Which of the turtles pictured do they think is Yertle? Why?

## After You Read

From a turtle who isn't satisfied with being king of the pond to a rabbit and a bear who can't help but argue about who's better than whom, this book teaches the value of restraint and humility. Explore these themes by asking the following questions.

◎ Why do you think Yertle wanted his throne to be higher and higher? What words do you think best describe Yertle?

◎ How do you think the other turtles feel about Mack?

◎ What do you think Gertrude McFuzz thought when she discovered the feathers weighed so much that she couldn't move? What lesson do you think she learned?

◎ Why do you think the rabbit and bear cared about being the best? What did they learn from the worm?

◎ If there were a sequel to this book, what do you think would be happening with the turtles, Gertrude, Mr. Rabbit, Mr. Bear, and the worm?

## Turtle Dominoes (Language Arts and Art)

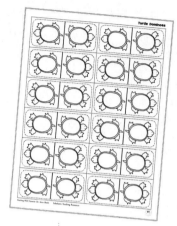

One of the things that make Dr. Seuss stories so colorful is the use of adjectives. Adjectives add color to writing, describing nouns with words like—in the case of *Yertle the Turtle and Other Stories*—*big*, *small*, and *droopy-droop*. Let students practice using adjectives with this creative version of Dominoes.

◎ Reread the story, noticing words that describe nouns, such as *young* (birdie), *big* (bear), *biggest* (fools), and *wonderful* (chair).

◎ Play a game of Turtle Dominoes to reinforce understanding of this part of speech. Give each child a copy of page 31. Have children cut out the dominoes and color the turtles. Encourage them to be creative in the details they include on their turtles. Some might be striped, others polka-dotted. Some might be checkered, some might be sad or glad. Some can have green eyes, brown eyes, or any other color eyes.

◎ Pair up children to play. Have one child start by placing a domino in the center. The other child chooses a domino that matches one of the turtles in some way, adds it to that turtle, and uses an adjective to describe how they are alike— for example, striped turtles. Have children continue taking turns in this way until they've linked as many dominoes as they can.

## Towering Turtles (Math and Science)

How many turtles did it take to make Yertle's throne? Use this question to initiate an investigation into numbers and the concept of balance. Let children guess how many blocks they could stack before their tower tumbles. Provide assorted blocks and let students work in small groups to test their ideas. Have students draw a picture of each tower as they construct it and record the total number of blocks stacked before they collapse. (They could do this with tallies.) Have them also jot down any strategies they use to try to build higher towers each time. Bring the class together to discuss results. Which strategies worked? Which didn't? Combine the most successful strategies from all groups to build a tower that is taller than all the others.

## Barked, Bellowed, Brayed (Language Arts)

The characters in these dialogue-rich stories don't just say things. They bark, bellow, bray, shout, snap, snort, thunder, howl, growl, groan, giggle, grunt, call, cry, chirp, yell, brag, and boast! Use the lively dialogue to explore the ways writers "talk" on paper, and help students learn to adjust their own use of language to communicate effectively.

◉ Reread the story, asking students to listen for characters talking. Discuss the ways the author helped the reader "hear" the ways in which the characters said things (by using words like *barked* and *bellowed*). Point out quotation marks in the story. Review the way writers use them to indicate that a character is speaking.

◉ On index cards, write words from the story that describe the way characters spoke, such as *howled, growled,* and *groaned* (one word per card). Place the cards in a bag. Write the same words on chart paper for reference.

◉ Bring students together in a seated circle. Let a volunteer select a card from the bag. Have this child say something that goes with the word on the card. Let children guess which word from the list best matches what the child said and how. Write the child's sentence and dialogue tag on a sheet of chart paper, having the child help place the quotation marks and comma—for example, "I can't believe we have homework," groaned James. Continue, letting other children take a turn in the same way.

## Higher, Better, Biggest (Language Arts, Math, and Art)

The stories in this book are about extremes—Yertle wants to be highest, Gertrude wants to have the best tail, Rabbit and Bear want to be the greatest at smelling and seeing (but are, in the end, the "biggest" at something else...). Use this as a starting point for an activity that strengthens vocabulary and number sense.

◉ List words in the story that compare people, places, or things. For example, the bear says he is "best of the beasts."

◉ Brainstorm other words that make comparisons—for example, *more, fewer,* and *less.* Record these on chart paper. Invite children to write and illustrate a sentence about the class that makes a comparison using any of these words. A child might show, for example, more children with lace-up sneakers than Velcro sneakers.

◉ Display the pictures. Discuss each comparison. Then challenge children to make new comparisons using each picture.

## Tip

▲▲▲▲▲

If students are wondering what to say to match the dialogue tags they choose, invite them to think about their day. Real life is a great writing resource!

## Book Link

*More, Fewer, Less*, by Tana Hoban (Greenwillow, 1998), explores number concepts with photographs that invite discovery on many levels. In a colorful photo of footwear, for example, children can notice more red shoes and boots than blue, fewer boots than shoes, and fewer shoes with zippers than with buckles. Children can revisit the photos again and again, making more discoveries with each new look.

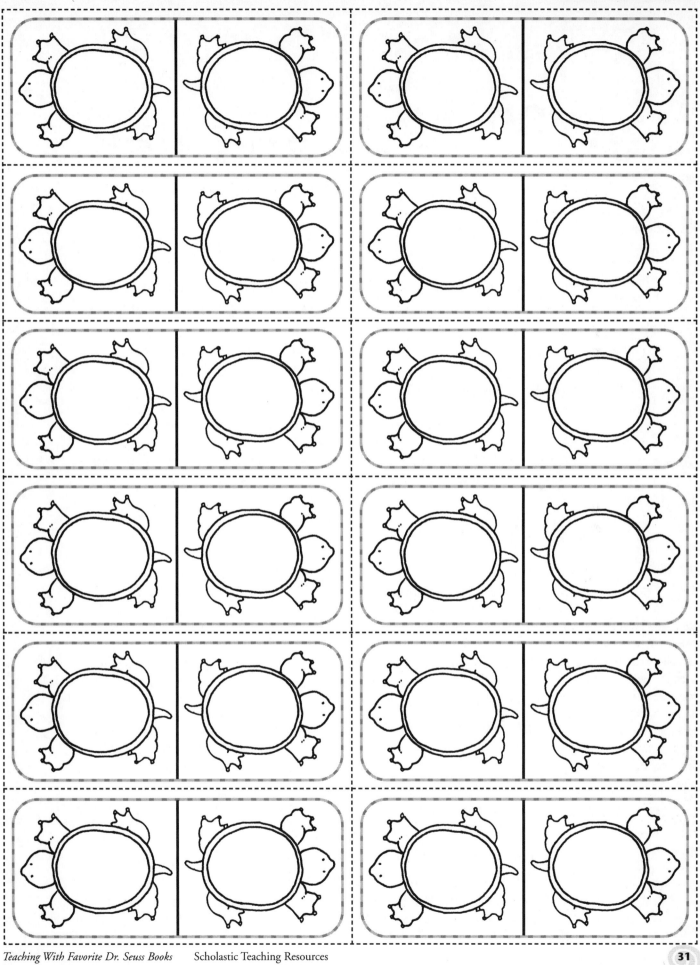

# Green Eggs and Ham

(RANDOM HOUSE, 1960;
RENEWED 1988)

Children will be chanting along to familiar words in this persuasive story as Sam tries with unrelenting persistence to convince his friend to try green eggs and ham.

## Before You Read

Direct children's attention to the character on the cover of the book. Judging from the facial expression, what does this character think about green eggs and ham? Let children imitate the expression. What are some words to describe the feelings that go with this face?

## After You Read

Children will want to talk about one thing when they finish reading this book—what it would be like to eat green eggs and ham. Keep the discussion going with questions that explore the way authors develop characters—on the inside and on the outside.

◎ At the beginning of the story, which character looks happy? (*Sam, page 3*) Which does not? (*the one on page 4*) How does this help you make a prediction about the story?

◎ What are some words that describe how the character in the tall black hat feels at different parts of the story? (*Revisit the illustrations, noticing that this character looks annoyed, worried, confident, angry, surprised, and even— eventually—happy.*)

◎ What are some of the ways Sam tries to convince his friend to eat green eggs and ham? Why do you think he doesn't give up?

◎ What are some words that describe a person like Sam? (*determined, persistent, stubborn*)

◎ How do you think both characters are feeling at the end of the story? How do you know?

## Counting On Sight Words (Language Arts and Math)

In the first four short lines of this story, children will encounter six words on the Dolch Basic Sight Vocabulary list (*that, I, am, do, not, like*). And two of those words appear three times each! As children commit some of the words in the story to memory, they can match them with the printed words, in time learning to recognize this sight vocabulary in other places and building reading fluency. To reinforce sight word recognition, combine a read-aloud of the story with this graphing activity.

◎ Choose a number of sight words that appear in the story—for example, *that, I, am, do,* and *not.*

◎ Write each word in large letters at the bottom of the chalkboard. Draw vertical lines between each word to create a graph.

◎ Assign children to each word. Have children stand next to their words at the chalkboard.

◎ Reread the story. Have children make a star (or write the word) in their column each time they hear it.

◎ Let children at the chalkboard take turns with a pointer, leading the class in reading each sight word as many times as it was noted. Count the number of times children heard each word and compare. Which word did they hear most often? Have them order the sight words, from most frequent to least frequent. Repeat the activity with a new set of sight words and a different group of children.

## Tip

▲▲▲▲▲

To strengthen classifying skills, let children cut out things that are green from magazines. Place them at a center with yarn for making a Venn diagram. Let children visit the center to practice sorting the green things. Have them describe their sorting rules on chart paper so that classmates can give them a try, too.

## Go Green! (Science and Language Arts)

Children may not have enjoyed a meal of green eggs and ham, but they're probably familiar with lots of other green foods. Brainstorm some, and then use the list to launch an activity that will challenge children's classifying skills and get them thinking about characteristics of foods they do—or don't—like.

◎ Invite students to name foods that are green—for example, beans, peas, broccoli, cabbage, celery, kale, green grapes, kiwi, and collards. Write the names for these foods on index cards (one per card).

◎ Let each child think of a way to classify green foods—for example, Green Foods I Like or Green Foods That Are Fruits—and write it on an index card.

◎ Make a large Venn diagram by overlapping two hula hoops (or forming overlapping circles with yarn). Place children's index cards facedown next to the Venn diagram and let a child randomly select two. Place one next to each circle.

◎ Let children take turns selecting an index card and deciding where it goes: in the overlapping section of the circles if it shares both characteristics, in one or the other labeled circles if it matches only one of the descriptions, and outside both circles if it does not belong in either. Continue with other green foods until they've all been classified. Let a child choose two new classification cards and repeat.

## Who Eats Eggs? (Math)

Use this story as a springboard for an activity that lets children learn more about each other, and reinforces graphing and data analysis skills.

◎ Take a quick survey: "Who has eaten green eggs? Who would like to?" Take a count for each question and compare.

◎ Take a second survey: "What is your favorite way to eat eggs?" Have students make graph markers to show their response (scrambled, fried, and so on). Children who don't like eggs can write "I do not like them!"

◎ Set up a graph on a large sheet of paper, writing the different ways to prepare eggs across the bottom and including a space for "I do not like them!" at the end. Have children take turns placing their graph markers in the appropriate column.

◎ Discuss the data, asking questions such as "How many more children would rather have their eggs [name one way] than [name another way]? Do more children in our class like or dislike eggs?"

◎ As a follow-up, invite children to gather the same information from family members. Create a second graph and compare the data. How are the graphs similar? How are they different?

## All About Eggs (Science, Language Arts, and Art)

Which animals lay eggs? Let children find out with an investigation that teaches the use of nonfiction text features.

◎ Brainstorm animals that lay eggs—for example, chickens, geese, turtles, fish, frogs, butterflies, and snakes.

◎ Let children work with partners to investigate one of the animals that lay eggs. Provide assorted materials for making models of the eggs. Clay is an obvious choice, but children might also paint small rocks, stuff small bags, or mold tissue paper and wrap with yarn or tape. Have children write captions to go with their models.

◎ To go further, have children create a page for a nonfiction book, drawing a picture of the egg, the baby animal that hatches, and the mother. Have them label each part, and write captions that include key facts.

◎ For a fun follow-up, write clues about eggs and the animals that lay them on slips of paper—for example, "I leave my eggs on a leaf. The leaf will be food for my babies when they hatch!" Glue pictures of corresponding animals to index cards. Place each clue in a plastic egg, and place eggs in a basket. Display animal cards nearby. Let children take an egg, "crack" it open, and match animals to eggs.

Book Link

After brainstorming with children animals that lay eggs, share a book to learn more, such as *Chickens Aren't the Only Ones*, by Ruth Heller (Price, Stern, Sloan, 1993). Follow up by asking children if they know any other animals to add to their list.

# One Fish, Two Fish, Red Fish, Blue Fish

(RANDOM HOUSE, 1960;
RENEWED 1988)

A fish with a car, a fish with a star, a fish that is sad, a fish that is glad...What else will children discover in this book about funny things? There's a Wump, a Zans, a Gox, a Gack, a Ying, a Yink, the Zeds, a Zeep, and lots more!

## Before You Read

Share the title of this book, writing it on the chalkboard and underlining the word *blue*. Play with rhyming words and spelling patterns by inviting children to suggest words that could replace *blue*—for example, *boo, true, moo, zoo, shoo, new,* and *few*. The words don't have to make sense. Silly words are just fine. Look at the words together. Which letters make the /o͞o/ sound?

## After You Read

Funny things are everywhere in this book! Let students take turns sharing their favorite funny things. Follow up with questions that further explore the story.

◎ Where are some of the places you can see funny things in this story? (*for example, in the water, on a tree, on a cliff, in an ear, in the park*)

◎ If you had Ish's dish to help you wish, what would you wish for?

◎ If a Yop likes to hop and a Zans opens cans, what do you think a Bling could do? (*for example, a Bling could swing*) How about a Whum? (*for example, a Whum might like to hum*)

◎ What are some funny things in your day?

## My Name Is... (Language Arts)

In the story, Ish has a dish on his hand. Students will have fun substituting their own name for *Ish* to come up with a new rhyme. Use children's word choices to teach sound-letter relationships and spelling patterns.

◎ Write the "Ish, dish" pair of sentences from the story on sentence strips. Cut apart the last word in each sentence (*Ish* and *dish*). Place the sentences in a pocket chart.

◎ Let children write their names on sentence strips and trim to size. Invite them to take turns replacing Ish's name with their own, and then replacing the word *dish* with something that rhymes with their name. Children can help each other out, being as silly or serious with their word choices as they like—for example:

> My name is Patrick. On my hand I have a hat trick.
> My name is Rose. On my hand I have a nose.

## Fast, Slow, High, Low (Language Arts and Art)

How many words can children find in the book to describe funny things? There's *fast, slow, high, low, thin, fat, red, blue, old, new, sad,* and *glad* for starters. Use the story as inspiration for a lesson on adjectives.

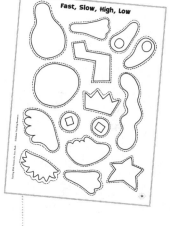

Fast, Slow, High, Low

◎ From the story, list adjectives and the words they describe—for example, *new fish, old fish, little bed,* and *hot sun.*

◎ Let children highlight words that name people, places, or things. Have them use a different color for words that describe each noun. Invite students to tell why they think authors use words like *new* and *old.* (*They help tell about something and add "color" to writing.*)

◎ Invite students to create their own "funny things" to describe. Give each child a copy of page 39 and a sheet of drawing paper. Have children cut out the pieces and arrange them any way they like to create a funny thing. When they are satisfied with their thing, they can glue the pieces in place. On a separate sheet of paper (or an index card), have students write a name for their funny thing and adjectives to describe it.

◎ Display the funny things and read aloud the descriptions, one at a time. Can children match each description to the corresponding thing?

## Two Feet, Four Feet, More Feet (Math and Art)

Use the picture on pages 12–13 of the book as a springboard for an activity that combines skip-counting, pre-multiplication, and patterns.

◉ Reread page 12. Let children point out some creatures with two feet. Can they find some with four? Six? Count by twos to extend the pattern. Can children find funny things with eight feet? More?

◉ Give each child a foot template to trace, or have them trace their own feet. Tack up a long sheet of mural paper. Have children arrange their feet in sets to create a pattern. It can be modeled on the one in the book (counting by twos) or on another pattern.

◉ When the pattern is complete, have children work together to make a creature to go with each set of feet. For example, if the feet are arranged in multiples of three (three feet, six feet, nine feet, twelve feet, and so on), have children add on to the feet to create a creature with three feet, one with six feet, and so on.

## Hop Like a Yop! (Movement)

Help children master left and right by letting them hop like a Yop. Designate one child to be the leader each day. You might give this child a crown to wear that has a Yop-like headpiece attached. At some point during a seated activity, have this child surprise the class by announcing that it's time to "hop like a Yop." Then have children stand and, on the leader's cue, hop from left to right and right to left, chanting each direction in turn. Continue hopping and chanting together until it's time to stop.

# Fast, Slow, High, Low

# The Sneetches and Other Stories

(RANDOM HOUSE, 1961;
RENEWED 1989)

**F**our short stories teach several valuable life lessons and one lesson that's just plain fun. Along the way, readers will meet some expressive characters, including the Star- and Plain-Belly Sneetches, a North- and South-Going Zax, almost two dozen Daves, and a pair of pale green pants that smile and say "Hi!"

## Before You Read

Both characters on the cover are wearing a similar expression. Invite students to describe the expressions and what the characters are feeling. Possibilities include smug, snooty, conceited, and arrogant. Let children imitate the characters' expressions to "try on" these feelings.

## After You Read

The characters in this book have much to say about life. Use the following questions to deepen students' understanding of the stories and to make connections to characters in other literature they know.

◎ Why do you think the Star-Belly Sneetches think they're better than the Plain-Belly Sneetches?

◎ What kind of a character do you think Sylvester McMonkey McBean is? (*for example, clever, cunning, tricky*) What are some clues?

◎ Has anyone ever behaved like a Sneetch with you? How did that make you feel?

◎ The South-Going Zax has a rule: "Never budge." Can you think of a rule that is more considerate?

◎ What was scary about the green pants? Why aren't they scary at the end of the story?

◎ How are some characters in other books you know similar to the characters in this book? (*For example, like the characters in "The Zax," Spinky, in* Spinky Sulks, *by William Steig, has a stubborn streak that gets in the way of other things.*)

## A Lot Alike (Social Studies and Language Arts)

Stars or no stars, the Sneetches were alike in many ways. Help students make a connection to people around them with an activity that builds an appreciation for the many ways people are alike.

◎ Revisit the illustrations that picture Sneetches. Ask students to name ways the Star-Belly Sneetches and Plain-Belly Sneetches are alike—for example, they are all yellow and they all have a tuft of hair on their head, a white band around their necks, two hands, two feet, and a beak.

◎ Divide the class into small groups. Set a timer for one minute, and challenge each group of children to list in that time as many ways as they can that they are alike.

◎ Bring students together to share their lists. Combine their ideas to create a class list of the things children have in common. Curly hair or straight, pizza-lovers or not, they're a lot alike!

## Star-Belly Sneetch Spelling (Language Arts)

The double -e in *sneetch* is just one way to spell a long -e sound. Use this word as a springboard for spelling instruction.

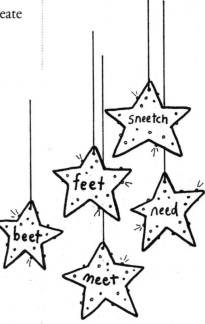

◎ Write the word *sneetch* on chart paper. Invite children to suggest other words that have a long -e sound. Record words that have an -ee spelling pattern under the word *sneetch*. Record words with other spelling patterns on another sheet of chart paper.

◎ Create a sparkly spelling display with the -ee words. Write each word on a star cutout. Punch a hole in each star, tie on a length of string or yarn, and dangle from the ceiling or a clothesline.

◎ Use highlighters in different colors to group remaining words by the letters that represent the long -e sound—for example, words with -ea, -ie, -ei, and -e. Set up a sheet of chart paper for each spelling pattern.

◎ Reread the story to focus on these sound-spelling patterns. Give each child a star cutout. Let children write the word *sneetch* on it. Reread the book, this time asking children to raise their stars when they hear a word with the long -e sound, including *beaches, we'll, treated, seems, keen, McBean, need, speed, guaranteed, three, each, me, money, we're, we, grief, he, eaches, precisely, removed, tummies, beaks, really, screaming, neither, beach,* and *teach.* (Some words appear more than once.)

◎ Add these words to the charts (unless they've already been suggested). Create spelling lists with the words, focusing on one spelling pattern at a time.

## Tip

▲▲▲▲▲

This activity lends itself well to teaching with Venn diagrams.

## Tip

▲▲▲▲▲

For a challenge, add one long -e word to the week's long -e spelling words that has a different long -e spelling. Give a bonus for spelling this word correctly!

## Feelings and Faces (Health)

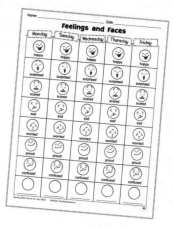

Use this activity to help children make connections with the characters in the book and become more aware of the many different feelings they have.

◉ Give each child a copy of the chart on page 43. Read the word that goes with each face.

◉ Revisit the book, and look for characters who show the different feelings represented on the chart. Discuss what was happening in the stories to make them feel this way.

◉ Each day, have children color in the faces that show the ways they feel. Do this for one week.

◉ At the end of the week, ask children to review their charts. Invite them to share something they discovered about themselves. Make connections to the story by asking children which characters they felt like at different times during the week.

## 23 Sons (Math)

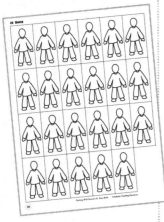

In "Too Many Daves," Mrs. McCave had 23 sons and she named them all Dave! Revisit the illustrations in the story to see what kinds of activities the Daves like to do (such as play baseball, sing, walk on stilts, and juggle). Then take the idea of 23 Daves further to strengthen math skills.

◉ Give each child a copy of page 44. Have children color in the kids and cut them out.

◉ Share a math problem based on the illustrations in the story—for example, "Two Daves are playing tennis, one is on stilts, and three are playing baseball. How many are not doing any of these things?"

◉ Ask children to use their cutouts to show the problem and the answer. Have them write the corresponding number sentences on a sheet of paper. (*To go with the above problem, for example, they might write 2 + 1 + 3 = 6; 23 − 6 = 17.*)

◉ Share other problems and let students suggest their own, too. Have them use the cutouts to show their answers and add the number sentences to their sheets. For example, to answer the question "How many pairs of Daves in 23?" students might arrange their cutouts in sets of two and then count the pairs. Are any Daves left over?

Name _____    Date _____

# Feelings and Faces

| Monday | Tuesday | Wednesday | Thursday | Friday |
|--------|---------|-----------|----------|--------|
| happy | happy | happy | happy | happy |
| surprised | surprised | surprised | surprised | surprised |
| scared | scared | scared | scared | scared |
| sad | sad | sad | sad | sad |
| worried | worried | worried | worried | worried |
| proud | proud | proud | proud | proud |
| confused | confused | confused | confused | confused |
| _____ | _____ | _____ | _____ | _____ |

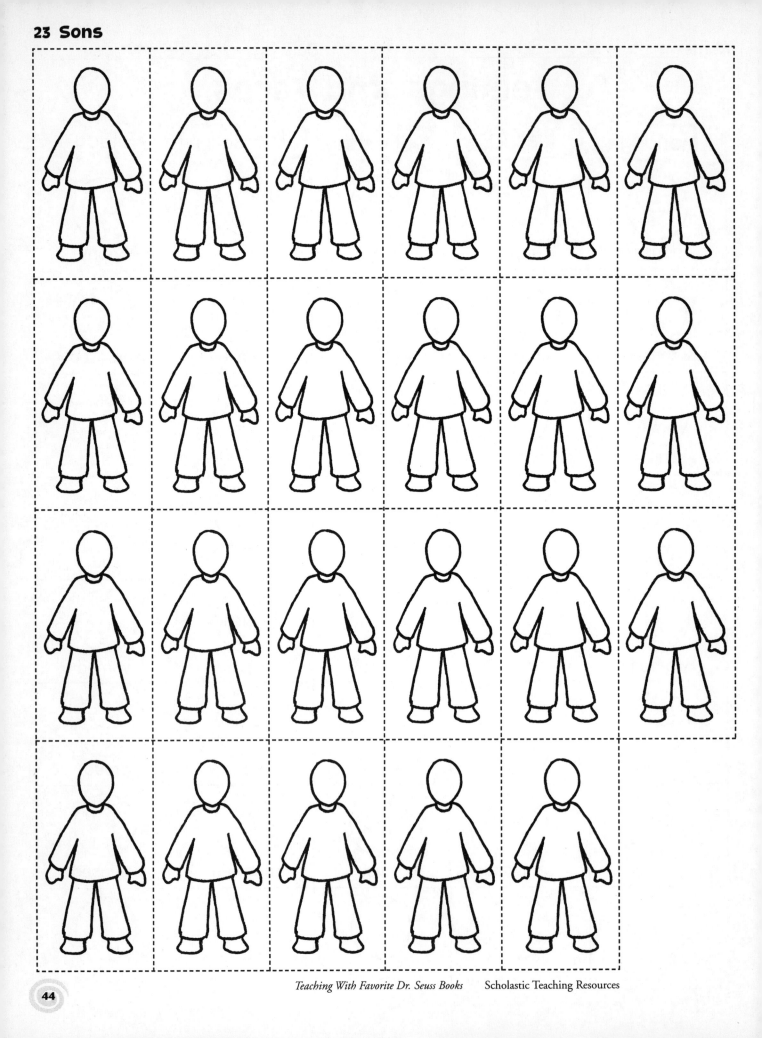

*Teaching With Favorite Dr. Seuss Books*    Scholastic Teaching Resources

# HOP on PoP

(RANDOM HOUSE, 1963;
RENEWED 1991)

This essential beginning reader builds vocabulary with predictable text and entertaining illustrations. From *up* and *pup* to *sister* and *brother*, the text zips right along to teach dozens of words.

## Before You Read

Who's having a good time in the illustration on the cover? Who might not be? Read the title: *Hop on Pop*. Ask students to change it so that the creatures skip instead of hop. Have them complete the new title: Skip on _____ . Try the same thing with other action words—for example, Swim on _____ and Sled on _____ .

## After You Read

Children have enjoyed this book for generations. Guide a discussion to explore what makes this book such a big hit.

◎ Why do you think, after more than 40 years, this book is still so popular?

◎ Which do you think was more fun: writing the words for this book or drawing the pictures? Why?

◎ There are lots of little words in this book. Why do you think the author added a couple of really big words near the end? (*Constantinople* and *Timbuktu*) What do you know about these words?

◎ What do you like about the ending of this story? Can you think of another good way to end the story?

## Circle Time Story   (Language Arts)

As a literacy and community-building activity, create a class retelling of *Hop on Pop* at circle time or morning meeting.

◎ Read the first two words of the story—*up* and *pup*. Replace the original sentence for these words with a new one—for example, "The pup jumped up."

◎ Pass the book to the child on your left. Have this child read the next set of words (*cup*, *pup*) and use them in a sentence.

◎ Continue, substituting new sentences for the ones in the book. As a challenge, replace the "big words" near the end of the story with other words. What are the biggest words students can think of?

## Mini Beginning Reader   (Language Arts and Art)

Take the simple text in this story further with an activity that lets children make their own mini beginning reader.

◎ After reading the book, revisit each page. Have children notice the setup of the words on the page: On most pages there are two (or three or four) rhyming words in large capital letters. Under these words is a sentence that uses those words.

◎ Give each child a copy of pages 48–49. Have children cut apart the mini-book pages, stack them in order, and staple to bind.

◎ Using *Hop on Pop* as a model, have students use the words on each page in a sentence and illustrate it.

◎ Children can add other pages as desired (for example, a page of "little words" like *if* and *it* and a page of "big words" like *Constantinople* and *Timbuktu*. Have them create a front and back cover, come up with a title, and staple to bind.

## Tip

▲▲▲▲▲

For children who are inspired to make more rhyming books in the style of *Hop on Pop*, stock a center with paper cut to mini-book size, a list of rhyming word pairs, and plenty of writing and art supplies. Be sure to allow time for students to share their tiny treasures!

## Top That Hop! (Math and Movement)

A large part of this book's charm lies in the silly connections it makes. Hopping on Pop is just one of them. Students will have fun hopping on Pop with an activity that strengthens measurement skills.

◎ Draw an outline of Pop on a sidewalk or safe area of pavement. Draw a starting line from which children will hop on Pop.

◎ Have children pair up to take turns hopping from the start line to Pop and measuring the distance. (They can use a nonstandard measure, such as a length of string, and then measure that with a tape measure.) Have them record their names and distances.

◎ Chart the distance of everyone's hop, from shortest to longest. Then use the data to explore math concepts such as range and average. What was the range of hops? By how much do they differ? What was the average distance hopped?

◎ Challenge children to explore other connections. For example, is there a correlation between the distance hopped and the height of the hopper?

**BIG
DIG**

_____

_____

①

**JAM
CLAM**

_____

_____

②

**SNAP
CLAP**

_____

_____

③

**BEST
PEST**

_____

_____

④

SOCK
CLOCK

_____

_____

⑤

TOT
SPOT

_____

_____

⑥

PLUNK
DUNK

_____

_____

⑦

HOW
COW

_____

_____

⑧

# Fox in Socks

(RANDOM HOUSE, 1965, RENEWED 1993)

As hard as Mr. Knox tries, he just can't keep up with Mr. Fox's tongue-twisting tricks and games, until the end, when Mr. Knox delivers some fun of his own.

## Before You Read

Read the "caution" on the book's cover. Then share the hint on the opening page of the book. What do children think these mean? Encourage them to use what they know about Dr. Seuss books to guess.

## After You Read

Phew! This story is a tongue twister from beginning to end. Reread the first four words of the book again. Write them on the chalkboard. Let children say them together, taking it slowly at first. Let them say the words again and again until they get their tongues "in trouble." Then use these questions to discuss the story—from the author's word choice to the surprise ending.

◎ What are some other words Dr. Seuss could have used on the first page in place of *socks*, *box*, and *Knox*? (*for example*, knocks, blocks, ox)

◎ What makes this a fun book to read aloud?

◎ Why do you think these kinds of sentences are called tongue twisters? Do you know a tongue twister? (Children might be familiar, for example, with "Peter Piper picked a peck of pickled peppers. How many pickled peppers did Peter Piper pick?")

◎ How do you think Mr. Fox feels for most of the story? How do you think Mr. Knox feels? Why?

◎ What is surprising about the way the story ends?

## Morning Message Tricks   (Language Arts)

Welcome students to school with a daily *Fox in Socks* tongue-twisting morning message.

◎ As part of the morning message, include a passage from the book. Start with a couple of the more simple lines. Work up to some of the longer "tricks" in the book.

◎ Invite children to practice the lines as they take care of their morning routines.

◎ When it's time for morning meeting, let children recite the lines they've learned. Use this activity as an opportunity to reinforce speaking and listening skills.

## Wait a Minute!   (Math)

Mr. Knox, looking quite exasperated, finally tells Mr. Fox to wait a minute. Children are often told "in a minute" or "just a minute" or "wait a minute." Help them see just how long a minute really is, and reinforce the concept of elapsed time (even if it's just one minute) with this fast-paced activity.

◎ Reread the part of the story in which Mr. Knox tells Mr. Fox to wait a minute. For emphasis, match the expression in your voice with the expression on Mr. Knox's face.

◎ Ask children how long they think a minute is. Record ideas on chart paper. Ask children what they think they could do in one minute—for example, straighten their cubbies, read a picture book, or write their name 20 times. Record these ideas, too.

◎ Set a timer for one minute. Select one of the things children think they could do in a minute, and have them begin when you say "Go!" (Start the timer.)

◎ At the end of one minute, say "Stop!" Discuss results. Could children accomplish the task in one minute? Did the minute seem longer or shorter than they thought?

◎ Repeat the activity with a few other tasks or activities. Then invite children to refine their ideas about what they could do in one minute, and repeat the activity with a new idea.

Book Link

*Telling Time With Big Mama Cat*, by Dan Harper (Harcourt Brace, 1998), includes a clock with movable hands so that readers can follow Big Mama Cat through her day—from waking up with a stretch at 6:00 to saying good night at 12:00. They can use the clock to show what happens in their day, too.

# Tick and Tock Pull-Through (Language Arts)

What rhymes with *tick* and *tock*? Make pull-through clocks to reinforce these common spelling patterns.

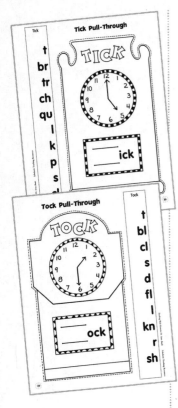

◎ Give each child a copy of pages 53 and 54. Have children cut out the clock patterns and decorate them, adding details to make their clocks as whimsical as they like. Help children cut the slits as indicated in the illustration.

◎ Have children cut out the letter list for each clock and thread them through the matching clock, as shown.

◎ Have children pull the strips through the clocks to make and read words.

◎ For more word-building fun, use the clock pull-throughs as models for making other kinds of pull-throughs. Look through the story to identify words that lend themselves to pull-throughs. For example, cut out a fox shape to make a pull-through that teaches the *-ox* word family (*fox, box, Knox, ox, lox,* and so on). Other ideas based on words in the book include: a duck-shaped pull-through to teach the *-uck* word family (*duck, cluck, muck, luck, stuck, tuck,* and so on); a tree-shaped pull-through to teach the *-ee* word family (*tree, bee, see, flee, glee, free,* and so on); a rose-shaped pull-through to teach the *-ose* word family (*rose, nose, hose, close, those,* and so on).

Tick

t
br
tr
ch
qu
l
k
p
s
cl

TICK

____ ick

# Tock Pull-Through

TOCK

ock

Tock Pull-Through

Tock

t

bl

cl

s

d

fl

l

kn

r

sh

*Teaching With Favorite Dr. Seuss Books*   Scholastic Teaching Resources

# The Foot Book

(RANDOM HOUSE,
1968)

Left, right, front, back...there are all sorts of ways to look at feet, and quite a few things to learn with them. This book cleverly connects feet with direction, color, number, position, possession, and other concepts.

## Before You Read

Introduce this book by asking students: "What do you know about feet?" Record their ideas on chart paper. Ask: "Do you think our class knows enough about feet to fill a book? What do you think Dr. Seuss has to say about feet? Do you think this story will be silly or serious? Why?"

## After You Read

After listening to this story, how many different ways to describe feet can students recall? (*red, black, small, big, and so on*) Let them list what they remember. Then continue with questions that build awareness of language patterns and encourage critical thinking.

◎ Why is *The Foot Book* a good title for this book?

◎ What's another title that would work for this book? (*for example,* Feet, Feet, Feet!, The Book About Feet, All About Feet, or Meet These Feet!)

◎ How many ways could we complete this sentence: [read aloud a sentence with a pair of rhyming words, leaving off the second rhyming word]? (Repeat this with several sentences in the book to explore patterns in the text.)

◎ How is this book like other Dr. Seuss books you've read? How is it different?

## Meet These Feet!
(Language Arts and Art)

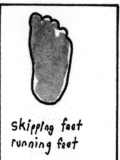

dancing feet
tapping feet

skipping feet
running feet

The characters in the story have feet that are wet, dry, high, low, red, black, slow, quick, small, big, fuzzy, and more. What words would students use to describe their feet? Give each child a foot tracing (of their own foot or of a template children trace and cut out). Have children decorate their foot tracing and then glue it to a sheet of plain paper. Ask children to add words that describe their feet or things they can do with their feet—for example, *wiggly feet* or *wide feet*. Display the pictures and let children match feet to their owners.

## Fishing for Feet (Math)

This book will surely inspire a closer look at feet. This game, based on the familiar card game Go Fish, explores attributes while strengthening observation, sorting, and classifying skills.

◎ Give each pair of children two copies of page 59. Have children cut out the cards and mix them up (both sets together).

◎ To play, each child takes five cards. The remaining cards are placed in a stack facedown between the children. Have children take turns asking each other for a card they need to make a match. Children must ask for the card by describing the foot's attributes—for example, "Do you have a foot that is fuzzy?" If the child being asked has a fuzzy foot card, he or she gives it to the other child and the match is placed faceup on the table. If not, the child replies, "Go fishing for feet." The other child takes the card on top of the stack. If this card makes a match with another card, the match is placed faceup on the table. If not, it's the other player's turn.

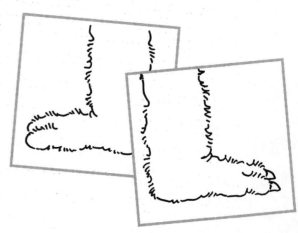

◎ Play continues until one player is out of cards.

## Left, Right (Math and Art)

The idea of left and right is an interesting—and challenging—one for young children. An object on one person's left will be on someone else's right, depending on where each is standing relative to the object. Yet a child's left foot is always left, no matter who is standing where. Explore the concept of left and right with this activity.

◎ Revisit the first few pages of the book. Ask children to identify the left foot and the right foot in the picture.

◎ Let children find the left and right feet in other pictures in the book. Discuss why this is confusing at times: Depending on the position of the feet, the left foot, for example, might be to the right on the page.

◎ Let children create their own creatures to learn more about left and right. Provide assorted craft supplies, such as pipe cleaners, feathers, felt, and yarn. Ask children to use the materials to create an animal that would fit right in with the characters in *The Foot Book*. Have children pay special attention to the feet. Will the left foot be up, down, high, low, front, back, red, black, fuzzy, or something else? How about the right?

◎ Once children have completed their creatures, have them complete these sentences: The left foot is _____ . The right foot is _____ .

## Tip

▲▲▲▲▲

Let children continue to explore the concept of left and right (at school or at home) with page 60. Give each child a copy. Together, notice the pictures. What are the feet doing in each? Let children complete the blanks to tell what's happening with the left and right feet. Have them create their own "left, right" picture in the last box and write sentences to go with it.

As an extension, invite
students to measure volume
of shoes—their own or an
assortment of other shoes.
Provide large-size
manipulatives, such as
number cubes or marbles.
You might count them out
in small cups by tens to
save time. Have children
predict how many will fit in
their shoe. Then have them
find out by adding a cup of
ten at a time, while a
classmate keeps a tally.

Book
Link

While you're on the subject
of feet, be sure to share **Not
So Fast Songololo**, by Niki
Daly (Aladdin, 1996). Set in
South Africa, this favorite
story shares a universal
message about the special
love between a
grandmother and child—
and a child's pure delight
in trading in a worn-out
pair of sneakers for a
dazzling new pair!

## Measuring Feet (Math and Language Arts)

Build measurement, problem-solving, and communication skills by posing
this challenge to children: How many ways can you find to measure a foot?

◉ Trace a foot on paper for each child (the child's foot or a foot pattern
you provide).

◉ Brainstorm ways people measure things. For example, ingredients to
bake a cake are measured in cups, teaspoons, and tablespoons. Height is
measured in feet and inches. Produce at the market is measured in
pounds. The free throw line in basketball is measured in feet.
Temperature is measured in degrees. The area of a floor is measured in
square feet or yards to find out how much carpet will cover it. Time is
measured in seconds, minutes, and hours.

◉ Now focus the idea of measurement on feet. Ask: "What is one way
people measure feet?" (*with a foot measure at the shoe store*)

◉ Provide small objects, such as dried beans and letter tiles, as well as yarn,
string, Wixi Stix, and ribbon. Invite children to measure their feet in as
many ways as they can. Have children record the measurements they
make, being sure to note the unit of measure.

◉ Bring students together to share results. List the many different ways
they measured their feet. Discuss reasons for using standard
measurement, especially for things like feet!

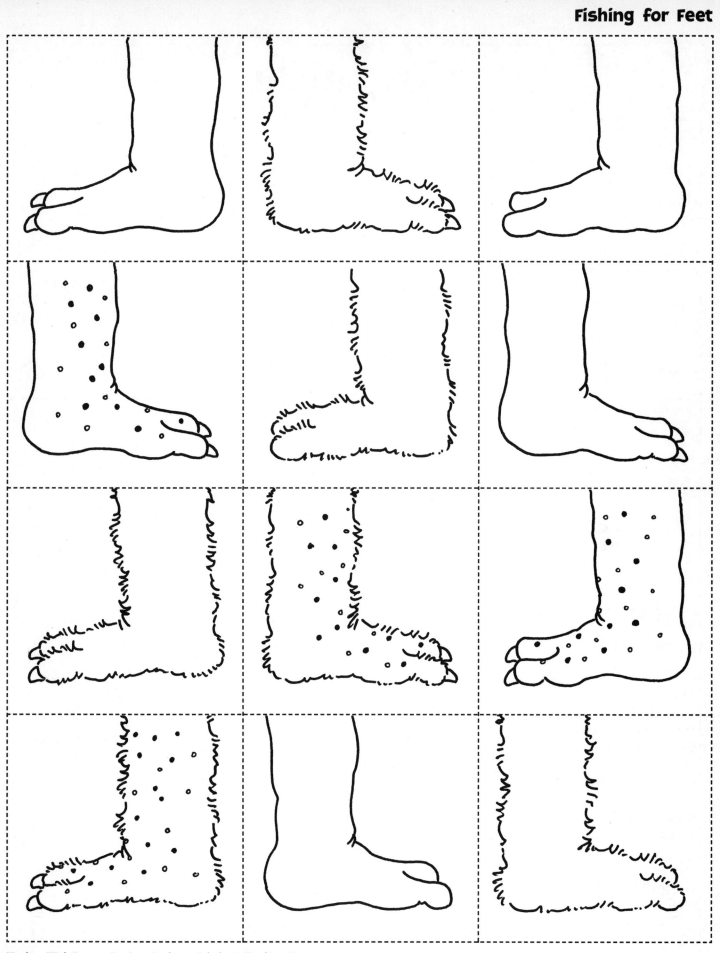

Name _____     Date _____

# Left, Right

The left foot is _____.
The right foot is _____.  ①

The left foot is _____.
The right foot is _____.  ②

The left foot is _____.
The right foot is _____.  ③

The left foot is _____.
The right foot is _____.  ④

The left foot is _____.
The right foot is _____.  ⑤

The left foot is _____.
The right foot is _____.  ⑥

*Teaching With Favorite Dr. Seuss Books*     Scholastic Teaching Resources

# The Lorax

(RANDOM HOUSE,
1971)

**W**hat was the Lorax? And what happened to it? The Once-ler knows, and will tell for 15 cents, a nail, and the shell of a snail. Told in classic Dr. Seuss rhyme, this story shares a universal message about caring that readers can carry with them long after the book is finished.

## Before You Read

Never heard of a Lorax? Invite students to look up the word in a dictionary. As they look, review dictionary skills. Which page would the word be on? Between which two words would they find the word they're looking up? Like many Dr. Seuss words, what they'll find is this word's not in the dictionary! Guide students in using the title of the book to decide what the corresponding part of speech is. (*noun*) Review what a noun is. (*person, place, thing, or idea*) Let students share their definitions for the word *Lorax*. Read the book for more information. Then let students refine their definitions.

## After You Read

This story of the Truffula Trees will inspire a lively discussion about stewardship of the earth. Use these questions as a guide:

◎ If you were the character on page 1 of this story walking down The Street of the Lifted Lorax, what would you think about this part of town? How do you think it got this way?

◎ Why do you think the Once-ler tells the story of the Truffula Trees?

◎ Did the Lorax's "sawdusty sneeze" get worse? (*Yes*) How do you know? (*It went from a sneeze to a cough, whiff, sneeze, snuffle, snarggle, and sniff.*)

◎ What do you think was causing the Lorax to sneeze and wheeze?

◎ What are some ways in which people can be greedy like the Once-ler was? If you were the Lorax, what would you say to them?

## Long Ago and Now (Language Arts)

Deepen students' understanding of character and setting with a closer look at the town and the Once-ler—now and long ago.

◉ Discuss what it means to compare (tell how things are alike) and contrast (tell how things are different).

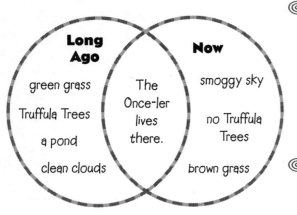

◉ Make a Venn diagram to compare and contrast the town now and long ago. In what ways is it the same? (*For example, the Once-ler still lives there.*) In what ways is it different? (*For example, long ago the town had green grass, a pond, clean clouds, Truffula Trees and Truffula Fruit, Brown Bar-ba-loots, and the Lorax. Now the grass is brown, the air is smoggy, the Truffula Trees are all gone and so are the Bar-ba-loots and the Lorax.*)

◉ Repeat the process of comparing and contrasting with the Once-ler. How is the Once-ler the same now as he was long ago? How is he different?

## Stopping the Chopping (Language Arts and Social Studies)

What happened when the Once-ler chopped down the first Truffula Tree? Make a cause-and-effect chain to explore story structure.

◉ Start a cause-and-effect chain on chart paper. Start with the Once-ler cutting down the first Truffula Tree. Continue with the Thneed that the Once-ler made from the tuft of the tree, the factory that was built to make more Thneeds from more trees, and so on.

◉ Discuss the chain. How did one thing lead to another?

◉ Make connections to students' lives by investigating the environment in their neighborhood (town, city, state, and so on). For example, are any animals' habitats being destroyed or endangered from development? Are streams or lakes being polluted? How is the air quality? Choose a topic to learn more about. Organize information in a cause-and-effect chain to look at what is happening and why. Plan a class stewardship project as a culmination.

## Tip

Invite students to pretend they're the Lorax. How would they convince the Once-ler to stop chopping down the trees? Encourage children to provide details that back up their positions.

## Gruvvulous Gloves (Language Arts and Art)

The Once-ler hides payments in his "gruvvulous glove." Revisit the picture that shows this special glove. Then let students practice creative writing skills and strengthen word choice with this art activity.

◎ Invite students to bring in favorite print advertisements. Discuss what makes these advertisements appealing or effective: Who is the target audience? How do you know? What words help sell the product?

◎ Challenge children to create equally effective print advertisements for something in the book—for example, the gruvvulous gloves, the Whispa-ma-Phone, a Thneed, Gluppity-Glup, Schloppity-Schlopp, or Truffula Seeds. As part of the process, provide mini-lessons on word choice. Notice the number of words in the advertisements students shared. Why is it important to choose each word carefully?

◎ Let children present their advertisements to the class. Encourage the audience to notice something effective about each ad.

## Counting Coins (Math)

The Once-ler charges 15 cents to tell what happened to the Lorax. Use this as a springboard to learn more about money and to encourage critical thinking.

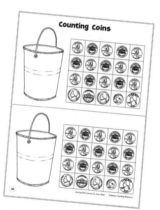

Counting Coins

◎ Give each pair of children a copy of page 64. Have children cut out the coins and bucket, then take turns being the Once-ler. The Once-ler "lowers" the bucket, and the other child counts out 15 cents and drops it in. The Once-ler counts the money and records the combination of coins. Children trade places and repeat the activity. Have children continue taking turns, recording as many different combinations of coins that equal 15 cents as they can.

◎ Bring children together to discuss the various coin combinations they used to pay the Once-ler—including 15 pennies, three nickels, two nickels and five pennies, one nickel and ten pennies, one dime and one nickel, and one dime and five pennies.

◎ Go further to explore the concept of giving change. Again, let children take turns being the Once-ler. This time, have children use a quarter to pay. Have the Once-ler make change. Discuss the various combinations children used to give change, including ten pennies, two nickels, one nickel and five pennies, and one dime.

Book Links

The Truffula Trees are a good reason to practice conservation. For more good reasons, share the Caldecott Award winner *A Tree Is Nice*, by Janice Udry (HarperCollins, 1956). Go further with some tree identification. *First Field Guide: Trees (National Audubon Society)*, by Brian Cassie (Scholastic, 1999), categorizes trees by the shape of their leaves. *A B Cedar: An Alphabet of Trees*, by George Ella Lyon (Orchard, 1989), features the leaves and fruit of trees from A to Z.

# Counting Coins

*Teaching With Favorite Dr. Seuss Books*   Scholastic Teaching Resources